SAM ALTMAN'S BOLD VISION FOR A SUPERINTELLIGENT FUTURE

The AI Revolution

How Artificial Intelligence Could Reshape Humanity and Transform Everything We Know

Alejandro S. Diego

Table of Contents

Introduction...4

Chapter 1: The Superintelligent Horizon....................7

Chapter 2: AI Teams – Personal Assistants of the
Future... 13

Chapter 3: AI and Global Prosperity........................20

Chapter 4: The Next Generation of AI Devices........ 29

Chapter 5: The Critics and Challenges....................38

Chapter 6: AI's Role in Shaping the Future.............49

Conclusion... 59

Introduction

In a world rapidly transforming through technological advancements, one innovation stands at the forefront of change—artificial intelligence. This book explores a vision that pushes the boundaries of what AI can achieve, one that looks not only at its present capabilities but at its future potential to reshape the very fabric of society. At the center of this vision is Sam Altman, a leader whose work with OpenAI has positioned him as one of the most influential voices in the AI revolution. His insights into the future of superintelligent AI go far beyond traditional expectations, offering a glimpse into a future where AI becomes an integral part of human progress.

The reason AI holds such significance today is clear. It is no longer a concept of the distant future but a technology that is evolving at breakneck speed. From simple automation tools to complex systems capable of learning and adapting, AI is now part of our daily lives. Governments, industries, and individuals are taking note, as this technology begins to impact everything from healthcare and education to entertainment and communication. With each new development, public interest grows, and the question on everyone's mind is: What comes next?

Sam Altman believes that the answer lies in superintelligence—an AI more intelligent than humans, capable of solving problems we have yet to even define. As the CEO of OpenAI, Altman has led efforts to push the boundaries of what AI can do. His vision is bold, imagining a future where AI is not just a tool but a partner in our growth, one that could revolutionize industries, improve quality of life globally, and tackle challenges that seem insurmountable today.

As this book unfolds, readers will explore Altman's ambitious predictions for AI's role in society. From the breakthroughs in medical science to the potential for solving global crises like climate change, the narrative will guide you through a world where AI is central to human progress. We'll also delve into the challenges and criticisms that accompany this vision, providing a balanced view of both the promises and the risks. Whether you're already familiar with AI or just beginning to understand its impact, this book offers a detailed and engaging exploration of the technology that is set to change everything.

Chapter 1: The Superintelligent Horizon

Sam Altman's prediction of superintelligence is nothing short of revolutionary. He envisions a world where artificial intelligence, in just a few short years, will surpass the intellectual capabilities of humans. This is not a far-off dream but a reality that he believes will unfold within the next decade. According to Altman, superintelligence—AI that is smarter, faster, and more creative than the brightest human minds—has the potential to tackle problems we can barely imagine today. This leap will fundamentally alter how we live, work, and engage with the world around us.

Altman's vision is rooted in the idea that human progress has always been tied to the growth of collective intelligence. Throughout history, humanity's most significant advancements have not come from individual genius but from our ability to share knowledge, collaborate, and build upon the discoveries of others. From early communities pooling resources to modern societies leveraging global communication networks, the power of collective intelligence has driven our evolution. Altman sees AI as the next logical step in this journey. With AI, he believes, we can move beyond the limitations of human collaboration and harness an unprecedented level of cognitive power.

Where human collective intelligence relies on communication, shared experiences, and the slow accumulation of knowledge, AI introduces a new dynamic. AI systems can process vast amounts of data, learn at incredible speeds, and provide insights that no single human—or group of humans—could ever achieve. Altman sees this as the key to unlocking a future where humanity can solve challenges that have long stumped us, from finding cures for diseases to mitigating climate change.

This transition from collective human intelligence to superintelligence represents a seismic shift in how we think about progress. For Altman, it's not just about creating machines that are smarter than us; it's about using those machines to amplify human potential. By collaborating with superintelligent AI, society could enter a new era of innovation and prosperity, one that pushes the boundaries of what we thought was possible.

Sam Altman's forecast places the arrival of superintelligent AI within a relatively short time frame—he anticipates that within the next decade, we could witness the emergence of AI systems that surpass human intelligence. This rapid timeline is driven by several key factors. The continuous advancements in computing power, fueled by breakthroughs in hardware, are one of the most crucial drivers. AI models require immense processing capabilities, and as companies invest in developing more efficient chips and infrastructure, the speed at which AI can evolve accelerates. Additionally, the increasing availability of vast datasets, combined with improvements in machine learning algorithms, means that AI systems are learning and improving at an exponential rate.

These factors are converging to create a scenario where superintelligence is not just a possibility but a near certainty.

As this future approaches, the implications for everyday life are profound. Superintelligent AI will not simply be an abstract concept reserved for scientific or technical circles—it will become a deeply integrated part of society, influencing everything from our daily routines to the global economy. Imagine AI systems capable of managing complex supply chains, optimizing urban infrastructure, or even solving traffic issues in real time. The ripple effects would be felt in every corner of life, transforming how we interact with the world.

The potential applications of superintelligent AI are vast, but some of the most impactful areas include healthcare, education, and industry. In healthcare, AI has the potential to revolutionize diagnosis and treatment. With access to enormous datasets, AI could analyze patient records, research data, and medical literature far more quickly than any human, offering highly accurate diagnoses and personalized treatment plans. Diseases that have long been difficult to treat, such as cancer or Alzheimer's, could see breakthroughs as AI-driven systems identify new patterns and solutions that were previously overlooked.

In education, AI could radically change how learning is delivered. Rather than a one-size-fits-all approach, AI could create personalized learning plans tailored to each student's strengths, weaknesses, and learning pace. This could democratize education, making high-quality learning accessible to individuals regardless of their geographic location or socioeconomic status. AI tutors, available around the clock, could provide feedback and guidance that adapts in real time to the needs of each learner.

Industry, too, would undergo a transformation. AI could optimize manufacturing processes, reduce waste, and improve efficiency across the board.

Entire sectors might shift as AI-driven automation takes over repetitive tasks, allowing human workers to focus on more creative and complex roles. Industries such as logistics, agriculture, and finance could see dramatic improvements in productivity, as AI systems predict trends, manage resources, and solve problems faster than ever before.

Altman's timeline is ambitious, but the factors driving AI development suggest that his predictions are not far-fetched. The coming years could usher in a new age where AI is not only a tool but a partner in human progress, helping us tackle challenges that have long seemed insurmountable.

Chapter 2: AI Teams – Personal Assistants of the Future

Sam Altman envisions a future where individuals are empowered by their own personal AI teams—sophisticated assistants designed to work together as specialized units, each focusing on different aspects of daily life. These AI teams would go far beyond the virtual assistants we know today, such as those that manage calendars or answer simple questions. Instead, they would consist of highly specialized systems, each one tailored to a specific area of expertise, working in unison to amplify human capabilities. Whether it's managing your health, optimizing your work productivity, or navigating complex financial decisions, these AI assistants would provide real-time, personalized support.

The beauty of this vision lies in how these AI teams would enhance human decision-making and problem-solving abilities. Imagine having a team of virtual experts available at your fingertips, constantly learning from your interactions, preferences, and habits. They would not just respond to commands but proactively analyze situations and offer solutions tailored to your unique needs. For example, if you're managing a health condition, your personal AI team could track your medical history, cross-reference global research, and coordinate with healthcare providers to create a customized treatment plan. All of this would happen seamlessly, in the background, with your AI team handling the complex logistics while you focus on living your life.

In education, personal AI teams could revolutionize the way individuals learn and grow. Each AI in the team would specialize in a different subject or skill set, allowing it to adapt lessons to the learner's pace and style. The AI could identify areas where the learner struggles and provide targeted exercises or alternative explanations, turning what used to be a generic learning process into a highly customized journey. This approach would foster deeper understanding and help individuals achieve mastery faster and more effectively than traditional methods.

These AI teams wouldn't just excel in specific domains but would collaborate to enhance overall decision-making and productivity. For instance, a financial AI assistant could work alongside a health-focused AI to provide advice on managing medical expenses or investments. Similarly, an AI designed to optimize productivity could analyze your daily habits and suggest changes to streamline your work processes, helping you achieve more in less time. These assistants would continuously adapt, learning from each other and from their human counterparts, constantly refining their recommendations and solutions.

Altman's vision emphasizes that these AI teams are not about replacing human judgment but about augmenting it. They would allow individuals to make better-informed decisions by offering insights, analyses, and solutions that would be difficult or impossible for a person to process alone. The result would be a future where human capabilities are expanded exponentially, thanks to the collaborative efforts of specialized AI working together to improve every aspect of life.

To understand the true potential of Sam Altman's vision for personal AI teams, consider how they might operate in everyday life. Imagine a scenario where an individual is managing a chronic health condition, such as diabetes. In this case, the person's AI team would consist of a healthcare-focused assistant that monitors vital signs, analyzes dietary habits, and keeps track of medications. This AI would work in real-time with another assistant focused on logistics, which could coordinate appointments with doctors and ensure prescriptions are filled on time. At the same time, a fitness-oriented AI could suggest personalized exercise routines based on the individual's current health status and daily activity levels. These AI systems would not only function independently but collaborate to provide a holistic approach to managing the person's well-being, seamlessly integrating different aspects of healthcare and lifestyle management.

In education, the potential applications are just as compelling. Consider a high school student struggling with mathematics. Instead of relying solely on textbooks or one-size-fits-all tutoring, their personal AI team could consist of a math tutor AI, designed to adapt its teaching style to the student's preferred learning method. This AI could analyze where the student encounters difficulties, offering tailored exercises and real-time feedback. Alongside this tutor, another AI focused on study habits might monitor the student's overall learning process, offering insights on when to take breaks, suggesting efficient study techniques, and even analyzing sleep patterns to ensure optimal cognitive function. Over time, this AI collaboration could help the student develop a more effective learning strategy that goes beyond subject mastery, fostering long-term educational success.

For career development, personal AI teams could be transformative. Imagine someone working in a fast-paced corporate environment, aiming for a promotion. A career-focused AI would help by continuously analyzing trends within the industry, identifying skills the individual needs to develop, and curating personalized learning resources like online courses or seminars. Meanwhile, a productivity AI might suggest changes to their work schedule, streamline workflows, and even identify patterns in task completion to increase efficiency. Another AI could focus on personal branding, recommending networking opportunities, enhancing online profiles, and providing insights on how to present oneself effectively to prospective employers or clients. Together, these AI assistants would support career growth, offering the tools and guidance needed to navigate complex professional landscapes.

Altman's vision is clear: AI teams are not meant to replace human capabilities but to enhance them. In each of these examples, the AI does not make decisions for the person but instead provides valuable insights, suggestions, and solutions that empower individuals to make more informed choices. The idea is not to create a future where humans are dependent on machines to function, but one where AI helps humans function more efficiently, intelligently, and creatively. AI becomes a trusted partner, handling the data-driven aspects of decision-making while freeing individuals to focus on what they do best—critical thinking, creativity, and personal engagement.

This emphasis on collaboration rather than replacement highlights Altman's belief that AI should work alongside humans, amplifying their abilities and helping them achieve more than they could on their own. In this future, humans remain at the center, with AI teams serving as powerful tools that complement our natural strengths.

Chapter 3: AI and Global Prosperity

Sam Altman envisions a future where AI serves as a driving force behind an era of abundance—one in which prosperity reaches unprecedented levels across the globe. Central to this belief is the idea that AI will significantly enhance efficiency and innovation in virtually every industry. From manufacturing to healthcare, the ability of AI systems to analyze vast amounts of data, optimize processes, and predict outcomes will allow businesses and industries to operate at a level of precision and speed that humans alone could never achieve. This increased efficiency could lead to lowered production costs, higher productivity, and, ultimately, an economy that grows faster and benefits a broader range of people.

The economic implications of this AI-driven world are immense. Altman believes that as AI continues to optimize industries, it could lead to a significant global economic boost. By automating repetitive tasks and optimizing complex workflows, AI has the potential to create a world where goods and services are produced at lower costs and distributed more efficiently, making them accessible to more people. This, in turn, could lead to higher living standards for populations worldwide, reducing poverty and inequality. Furthermore, with AI handling much of the logistical and data-driven work, human creativity and innovation could flourish, as people are freed from mundane tasks and able to focus on more meaningful and creative pursuits.

Beyond economic growth, Altman is confident that AI will also lead to breakthroughs in fields that have long been considered insurmountable. In medicine, for example, AI could revolutionize how we understand, diagnose, and treat diseases. By processing enormous datasets from medical research, clinical trials, and patient histories, AI could uncover patterns and solutions that have eluded scientists for decades. This could lead to the discovery of new drugs, personalized treatments tailored to individual genetic profiles, and even early detection systems for diseases that are currently difficult to diagnose, such as cancer or Alzheimer's.

The potential for AI-driven innovation extends beyond medicine. In the field of physics, AI systems could assist researchers in solving complex equations, testing theories, and even making new discoveries in areas like quantum mechanics and astrophysics. These advancements could open up new possibilities for technology development, potentially leading to breakthroughs in energy production, space exploration, and material science. By handling the tedious calculations and data analysis, AI would allow physicists to focus on deeper theoretical work, accelerating the pace of discovery.

Perhaps one of the most pressing areas where AI could make a transformative impact is climate change. The scale and complexity of this global challenge require solutions that go beyond human capability, and Altman sees AI as the key to unlocking these solutions. AI could be used to model climate patterns with far greater accuracy, predicting the effects of different interventions and helping governments and industries make more informed decisions about how to reduce emissions and mitigate environmental damage. Additionally, AI could play a crucial role in developing new clean energy technologies, optimizing resource usage, and creating more sustainable agricultural and industrial practices.

Altman's vision of a world of abundance is rooted in the belief that AI, when harnessed properly, will be a tool for collective human advancement. It won't just be about solving individual problems but about creating a ripple effect of prosperity, innovation, and discovery that elevates society as a whole. While there are challenges to overcome, particularly in ensuring that this abundance is distributed equitably, Altman remains optimistic that AI has the potential to lift humanity to new heights.

As artificial intelligence continues to advance, Sam Altman foresees significant economic shifts that will reshape industries and open up new markets, ultimately improving global living standards. AI's ability to enhance efficiency and innovation across sectors could lead to the restructuring of traditional industries in profound ways. For example, in manufacturing, AI-powered automation could handle production processes with incredible speed and precision, reducing errors, minimizing waste, and lowering costs. This shift could make goods more affordable and accessible, creating a more efficient global supply chain that benefits both producers and consumers.

In industries like agriculture, AI could revolutionize how food is grown, harvested, and distributed. AI systems could analyze soil conditions, predict weather patterns, and optimize crop yields with pinpoint accuracy, helping farmers produce more food with fewer resources. Similarly, in logistics, AI could streamline the movement of goods, identifying the most efficient routes, reducing transportation costs, and ensuring that products reach consumers faster. This level of optimization could lead to the creation of new markets, particularly in emerging economies where AI could help bridge gaps in infrastructure and development.

AI's impact on the job market is another critical aspect of these economic shifts. While some fear that automation could eliminate jobs, Altman believes that AI will also create new opportunities by driving innovation and creating demand for new skills. Just as past technological revolutions gave rise to entirely new industries and job categories, AI could open doors for new forms of work that were previously unimaginable. Fields like AI maintenance, ethical oversight, and AI-driven creative industries could become major sources of employment, providing opportunities for people to contribute to an increasingly AI-integrated world.

However, while Altman remains optimistic about AI's potential to uplift global living standards, he is acutely aware of the challenges that come with it. One of the primary concerns is the risk that AI could become an exclusive tool for the wealthy and powerful, exacerbating existing inequalities. Developing and deploying advanced AI systems requires substantial resources—high-performance computing infrastructure, vast amounts of data, and significant energy consumption. Without careful planning and equitable distribution, there is a danger that only those with access to these resources will benefit from AI's capabilities.

Altman stresses the importance of scaling up infrastructure to make AI widely accessible. If access to the technology is concentrated in the hands of a few large corporations or nations, it could create a world where the gap between the wealthy and the poor widens even further. This would not only lead to social and economic disparities but could also spark conflicts over control of AI resources. To prevent this, Altman advocates for policies that promote fairness in AI distribution and ensure that its benefits reach all levels of society.

Another challenge is the infrastructure required to support widespread AI adoption. As AI becomes more integrated into daily life, the need for powerful computing systems, energy resources, and data centers will grow exponentially. Altman recognizes that without sufficient investment in these areas, AI could become a scarce resource, available only to those with the means to access it. To avoid this scenario, he emphasizes the importance of investing in infrastructure that can meet the demands of an AI-driven future while keeping costs low enough to make AI accessible to everyone.

In addition to infrastructure, there are concerns about how data is collected and used by AI systems. Since AI thrives on vast amounts of information, access to data becomes a critical factor in determining who can develop the most powerful systems. If large corporations or governments control the majority of this data, they may hold a monopoly on AI innovation, further limiting opportunities for smaller entities and individuals. Altman's vision, therefore, includes a push for more open and transparent data-sharing practices, ensuring that AI development is not concentrated in the hands of a select few.

In sum, while AI holds immense potential to restructure industries and improve global living standards, these benefits must be managed carefully to avoid deepening inequalities. By investing in infrastructure, creating fair access to data, and ensuring that AI resources are shared equitably, Altman believes we can harness AI's transformative power for the benefit of all. The key is to create a balanced approach that ensures AI's advantages are distributed across society, rather than becoming the privilege of a few.

Chapter 4: The Next Generation of AI Devices

Sam Altman's vision for AI doesn't stop at software; it extends into the realm of hardware, where he's teamed up with Jony Ive, the legendary designer behind Apple's most iconic products, to create a revolutionary AI device. Ive's design genius, responsible for shaping the iPhone, iPad, and Apple Watch, is now being applied to a new frontier: seamlessly blending AI with sleek, intuitive hardware. This collaboration marks a significant step toward creating a future where AI is not just a tool accessed through abstract systems but a tangible part of daily life, integrated into devices that feel as natural to use as a smartphone or laptop.

Altman and Ive's partnership is built on the idea that AI should be not only functional but also accessible and user-friendly. Their goal is to design a device that redefines how humans interact with technology, making AI an invisible yet powerful presence in everyday life. The focus is on creating something that feels personal and intelligent, a device that understands the user's needs and adapts to them seamlessly. While many of the details about the device are still under wraps, the concept is clear: a new kind of interface that brings AI closer to users in a way that feels effortless and intuitive.

The brilliance of Jony Ive's design approach lies in his ability to create devices that are both aesthetically beautiful and functionally revolutionary. He has a unique talent for making complex technology feel simple, something that is essential for an AI-driven device meant to integrate seamlessly into everyday life. By working together, Altman and Ive are looking to craft a product that doesn't just showcase AI's capabilities but makes those capabilities feel second nature to users. Imagine a device that you don't need to learn how to use, because it intuitively learns from you—adapting to your habits, preferences, and routines without requiring explicit commands or instructions.

This seamless integration of AI into hardware represents a shift in how we will engage with technology. Rather than interacting with AI through voice assistants or cloud-based software, this device could bring AI into a more physical, intimate form, possibly even something wearable or embedded into environments like homes and offices. The emphasis is on creating a user experience where AI doesn't feel like a distant, external force but a natural extension of the human mind. Whether it's through a touchscreen device, wearable tech, or an entirely new form factor, the hardware will embody the same principles of simplicity and elegance that have defined Ive's career while pushing the boundaries of what AI can offer.

This partnership signals a shift toward a future where hardware and AI are not separate entities but parts of a cohesive whole. By integrating AI into everyday objects, Altman and Ive aim to create a new kind of interaction, where the technology doesn't just respond to commands but anticipates needs, offering suggestions and solutions that feel organic and timely. The device could enhance productivity, creativity, and even personal well-being, functioning as a constant companion that evolves with the user over time.

In redefining the relationship between humans and machines, this collaboration could have far-reaching implications for how we live and work. The device could become a central hub of daily activities, making AI not only more accessible but more intuitive, a part of the flow of life rather than something we consciously use. Altman and Ive's combined vision promises a future where the boundaries between human capabilities and AI's potential are blurred, creating a new era of technology that feels more human than ever before.

While the exact details of the device that Sam Altman and Jony Ive are developing remain closely guarded, we can speculate on its possible features based on Altman's vision of a personalized and intelligent user experience. The device would likely be far more than just another gadget; it could serve as a deeply integrated personal assistant, powered by advanced AI systems that adapt and evolve with the user. Imagine a device that doesn't merely respond to input but anticipates needs, offering suggestions, insights, and solutions in real time without requiring constant prompts or commands.

One possible feature is that this device could act as an AI hub, consolidating multiple aspects of a user's life into a seamless experience. It might manage everything from daily schedules to long-term goals, tracking health metrics, financial data, and personal preferences to offer tailored advice and actions. For instance, if connected to health monitoring wearables, it could provide suggestions for improving well-being, from recommending diet adjustments based on biometric feedback to scheduling doctor appointments when needed. In education or work, it could curate personalized learning materials or streamline workflows by predicting tasks and optimizing productivity.

The device could potentially be highly intuitive, employing natural language processing to engage in conversations that feel more human-like and less mechanical. It might possess advanced voice recognition or even facial recognition capabilities, allowing it to understand emotional states and adapt its responses accordingly. This would further enhance its personal nature, making interactions feel more like collaborating with a trusted companion than using a machine.

Its form could be something entirely new, given Jony Ive's reputation for reinventing the physical designs of technology. Building on the sleek and minimalist aesthetic that made the iPhone and Apple Watch iconic, the device could be slim, portable, and tactile, perhaps incorporating a flexible, foldable display that adjusts depending on use or a seamless touchscreen with no visible buttons. Alternatively, it might take a more integrated form, such as wearable tech like smart glasses or even jewelry, blurring the lines between fashion and functionality while making AI an even more constant presence in the user's life.

The design philosophy behind this device would certainly follow the principles that have made Apple products so successful—combining aesthetic beauty with functional brilliance. Jony Ive's creations are known for their simplicity, a "less is more" approach that eliminates unnecessary complexity while ensuring that each element serves a purpose. This device will likely follow a similar path, stripping away traditional notions of hardware design to create something clean, intuitive, and elegant. Every detail would be considered, from the feel of the materials to the responsiveness of the interface, ensuring that the device is not just efficient but also pleasurable to use.

Moreover, the interaction between hardware and AI will likely be seamless, with the AI embedded so deeply into the device that it becomes almost invisible. Users wouldn't need to think about how the technology works or worry about complicated interfaces—the device would simply "know" and respond accordingly. This level of integration would elevate the experience to something that feels personal, intimate, and natural, reflecting both Altman's vision for intelligent AI and Ive's mastery of thoughtful, human-centered design.

In essence, this device would likely be a blend of the familiar and the revolutionary, with a sleek, modern design that draws from the best of past innovations but pushes forward into new territory. It could redefine what it means to interact with technology, making AI not just an occasional tool but a constant companion, effortlessly woven into the fabric of daily life. Through this partnership between Altman and Ive, we may see a device that reshapes our relationship with AI, making it feel less like a distant, futuristic concept and more like an intuitive, indispensable part of our everyday experience.

Chapter 5: The Critics and Challenges

While Sam Altman's vision for superintelligent AI is bold and filled with optimism, it has not been without its critics. AI experts like Gary Marcus have expressed skepticism about the feasibility of such a sweeping transformation. Marcus, known for his critiques of the limitations of deep learning, has questioned whether Altman's predictions about AI solving humanity's most complex problems and ushering in an era of global prosperity are grounded in reality or overly optimistic. These critics argue that while AI has made impressive strides, the gap between current AI capabilities and true superintelligence is far wider than Altman suggests.

One of the main critiques revolves around the fact that current AI systems, even the most advanced, are largely built on deep learning algorithms. These algorithms, while powerful, are based on pattern recognition rather than true understanding or reasoning. Deep learning excels at tasks like image and speech recognition, where it can process vast amounts of data and identify patterns. However, it lacks the ability to generalize knowledge in a human-like way. AI systems are still limited in their capacity to apply learned information across different contexts, which is a fundamental characteristic of human intelligence.

Gary Marcus and others have pointed out that while deep learning has led to breakthroughs in narrow AI applications, it falls short when it comes to achieving the kind of broad, adaptable intelligence required for superintelligence. Current AI models can perform well on tasks they've been specifically trained for but struggle when faced with novel situations that require common sense, reasoning, or an understanding of cause and effect. For true superintelligence to emerge, AI would need to not only process information but also comprehend it at a deeper, more conceptual level—something today's systems are far from achieving.

Another limitation is the reliance on massive datasets. Deep learning requires vast amounts of data to train models, which presents several challenges. First, there's the issue of data quality—AI systems are only as good as the data they are fed, and biases or inaccuracies in datasets can lead to flawed outcomes. Second, the sheer scale of data required means that only a handful of companies and institutions with access to vast resources can push AI development forward. This leads to concerns about monopolization of AI technology and the concentration of power in the hands of a few tech giants, as well as about the sustainability of such resource-intensive processes.

Moreover, deep learning models are often considered "black boxes." While they produce accurate results in many cases, understanding exactly how they arrive at those results can be opaque even to their creators. This lack of transparency raises concerns about trust, accountability, and the potential for unforeseen consequences, especially as AI begins to play a larger role in critical sectors like healthcare, finance, and governance. Critics argue that without a more transparent and interpretable form of AI, the widespread integration of these systems could be risky.

Another challenge on the path to superintelligence is developing AI that can exhibit true reasoning abilities. While there has been progress in areas like natural language processing and machine learning, AI still lacks the ability to engage in the kind of abstract reasoning that humans use to solve complex problems. Understanding context, navigating ambiguity, and applying knowledge flexibly are still major hurdles for AI development. Until AI can replicate this kind of cognitive flexibility, critics argue, the dream of superintelligence remains distant.

In addition, there are concerns about the ethical and societal implications of pursuing superintelligent AI. Critics warn that if the technology does indeed become as powerful as Altman envisions, there could be unintended consequences, from job displacement to the misuse of AI in warfare or surveillance. The rapid pace of AI development has outpaced the creation of ethical frameworks and regulatory structures, raising questions about whether society is truly prepared to handle the potential risks associated with superintelligence.

In summary, while Altman's vision of AI transforming the world is compelling, skeptics like Gary Marcus highlight the significant challenges that remain. The limitations of deep learning, the need for transparency, the gap in reasoning abilities, and the ethical considerations surrounding AI development are all critical points of concern. While AI continues to advance, the road to superintelligence is likely to be more complex and fraught with obstacles than some of its proponents may suggest. Altman's vision may represent the future, but it is one that will require overcoming substantial technological, ethical, and societal challenges before it can be realized.

The promise of AI's future, as envisioned by Sam Altman, comes with inherent risks, particularly in terms of security and ethical considerations. One of the most telling examples of these risks emerged when Altman's OpenAI-related accounts were hacked in a crypto scam. Hackers exploited the increasing public interest in AI and cryptocurrencies, promoting a fake token called "OpenAI" in an attempt to steal crypto wallet credentials from unsuspecting users. This incident wasn't isolated, as other OpenAI employees, including high-profile researchers, have also been targeted in similar attacks. These security breaches serve as a stark reminder of the vulnerabilities that come with an AI-driven world, especially as digital systems become more integrated into every aspect of life.

As AI becomes more pervasive, the scope of potential threats expands. The same AI systems designed to enhance security or optimize financial transactions can be used by bad actors for malicious purposes, such as creating deepfakes, automating large-scale cyberattacks, or engaging in social engineering schemes. In Altman's future, where AI is deeply embedded in everything from healthcare to personal finance, these vulnerabilities could pose significant risks to both individuals and society as a whole. The potential for misuse, whether through criminal hacking or even state-sponsored cyber espionage, highlights the need for robust security frameworks to protect AI systems and the data they manage.

Moreover, ethical concerns are closely tied to the rapid development of AI. As AI systems take on more critical roles, from decision-making in healthcare to predictive policing, ensuring they operate fairly and transparently becomes a pressing issue. Bias in AI algorithms, lack of accountability, and the opaque nature of many machine learning models all contribute to potential ethical pitfalls. If not properly addressed, these issues could undermine trust in AI technologies and exacerbate social inequalities.

Beyond the realm of security and ethics, Altman's vision also raises important questions about the future of work. AI's ability to automate tasks and streamline processes could lead to significant disruptions in the labor market. Certain jobs, particularly those that involve repetitive or data-driven tasks, are at high risk of being replaced by AI systems. Industries such as manufacturing, logistics, and retail are already seeing the effects of automation, with AI and robotics taking over roles once performed by humans. As AI continues to evolve, this trend is likely to expand into more complex fields, such as legal work, financial services, and even creative industries.

The potential for widespread job displacement is a major concern for many critics of AI development. If AI can perform tasks more efficiently and cost-effectively than humans, businesses may increasingly turn to automation, leading to a reduction in the demand for human labor. This could have devastating effects on workers, particularly those in low-skill or middle-skill positions, who may struggle to find new employment in a rapidly changing economy. The resulting economic inequality could deepen social divides, creating a world where those with access to AI and high-level skills thrive while others are left behind.

However, Altman and other AI proponents argue that while certain jobs may disappear, AI will also create new opportunities. Much like the Industrial Revolution, which transformed the labor market but also spurred the creation of entirely new industries, AI could lead to the emergence of new fields that we can't yet fully envision. Jobs in AI development, maintenance, and oversight are just a few examples of roles that could expand in an AI-driven economy. Moreover, as AI takes over mundane and repetitive tasks, humans may be free to focus on more creative, strategic, and interpersonal work—roles that require skills AI cannot yet replicate.

Education and reskilling will be critical in this new landscape. To ensure that workers are not left behind, governments, educational institutions, and businesses will need to invest in training programs that help people adapt to the changing job market. This could involve not only teaching technical skills but also emphasizing soft skills like critical thinking, problem-solving, and emotional intelligence, which will become increasingly valuable in a world where AI handles more of the routine work.

In conclusion, while Altman's vision of an AI-powered future offers the promise of greater efficiency, innovation, and prosperity, it also brings with it significant security and ethical challenges. The recent hacking incidents involving OpenAI accounts underscore the risks of a highly interconnected digital world, where bad actors can exploit vulnerabilities for their own gain. At the same time, the potential for social and economic disruption looms large, with AI threatening to displace jobs even as it creates new opportunities. Addressing these challenges will require careful planning, robust security measures, and a focus on education and reskilling to ensure that the benefits of AI are shared broadly and equitably.

Chapter 6: AI's Role in Shaping the Future

Sam Altman envisions a new era for humanity, which he calls the "Intelligence Age." This concept marks a profound shift in the way society will function, with AI playing a central role in amplifying human capabilities and addressing the most pressing challenges facing the world. The Intelligence Age goes beyond the digital and industrial revolutions, signaling a future where AI systems not only assist in performing tasks but also drive unprecedented progress across various sectors of society. Altman believes that as AI evolves toward superintelligence, we will enter a period where human potential is expanded, enabling new levels of innovation, problem-solving, and global prosperity.

In this Intelligence Age, AI will function as the bedrock of society, transforming how we interact with technology, make decisions, and tackle complex issues. Altman's vision isn't limited to enhancing efficiency or automation; it's about AI becoming a fundamental part of the human experience. This new era, powered by AI's ability to process vast amounts of data and learn at incredible speeds, will open doors to possibilities that were once out of reach. From medicine and education to industry and space exploration, AI will be woven into the fabric of everyday life, reshaping our world in ways that go beyond our current understanding.

One of the most audacious aspects of Altman's vision for the Intelligence Age is the belief that AI will help humanity solve its greatest challenges—problems that have stumped scientists, policymakers, and leaders for generations. One of the most significant areas where AI could make an impact is climate change. Altman suggests that AI could be used to develop and implement innovative solutions to reduce carbon emissions, optimize energy consumption, and model climate patterns with greater accuracy. By providing insights into how ecosystems interact, AI could offer new strategies for mitigating environmental damage and developing sustainable practices in agriculture, energy, and manufacturing. AI's potential to accelerate the shift toward renewable energy could be critical in reversing the damaging effects of global warming.

Altman also points to AI's potential role in space exploration and even space colonization. As the complexity of space missions increases, AI could be instrumental in solving problems that require vast computational resources and adaptive decision-making in real-time. From optimizing space travel logistics to developing sustainable life-support systems, AI could pave the way for humans to explore and eventually colonize other planets. This vision aligns with Altman's broader belief that AI will allow humanity to take on challenges that were previously unimaginable, pushing the boundaries of our achievements beyond Earth.

In the realm of scientific discovery, Altman foresees AI unlocking advancements in fields like physics, biology, and chemistry. One of the most exciting possibilities is the idea that AI could help unlock all of physics, solving fundamental questions about the universe that have puzzled scientists for centuries. By analyzing immense quantities of data and running simulations far beyond human capability, AI could provide breakthroughs in understanding everything from quantum mechanics to the origins of the universe. These discoveries could lead to new technologies and energy sources that could fundamentally change life on Earth.

In medicine, AI could accelerate the discovery of new drugs, improve diagnostics, and create personalized treatment plans based on individual genetic profiles. Altman's vision includes AI systems that not only aid in identifying diseases early but also predict health outcomes and offer tailored interventions before problems even arise. This proactive approach to healthcare, powered by AI's ability to analyze complex biological data, could lead to a healthier global population, with diseases like cancer and Alzheimer's becoming far more manageable or even curable.

Altman's concept of the Intelligence Age is one of optimism, where AI is the key to unlocking solutions to problems that humanity has long struggled to overcome. From fixing climate change to enabling space colonization and advancing scientific knowledge, AI offers the potential to drive humanity into a new era of progress. However, achieving this vision will require careful management of AI's development and application to ensure that these breakthroughs benefit all of society and not just a select few. The Intelligence Age, as Altman sees it, is a time of opportunity and growth, where AI becomes the ultimate tool for pushing the boundaries of human potential and solving the world's most daunting challenges.

As Sam Altman envisions a future powered by superintelligent AI, one of the critical elements that will make this transformation possible is infrastructure. The future of AI, particularly at the scale Altman predicts, requires enormous computational power, more energy resources, and larger data centers. These infrastructure needs form the backbone of AI development, allowing AI systems to process vast amounts of data, run complex algorithms, and continuously learn from their interactions. Without this robust infrastructure, the vision of AI solving humanity's greatest challenges and ushering in the Intelligence Age would remain unattainable.

At the heart of this infrastructure challenge is the sheer scale of computational power required. AI models, especially those based on deep learning, need enormous amounts of processing power to function effectively. Training AI models involves running thousands, if not millions, of simulations, each requiring significant computing resources. As AI systems grow more advanced and their applications expand, the demand for faster, more efficient processors will only increase. Companies like OpenAI are already investing heavily in custom-designed chips and hardware to meet these needs, but scaling this across the entire world is no small feat.

This computational demand is closely tied to the need for greater energy resources. AI models are not only computationally intensive but also energy-hungry. Running massive AI systems and data centers consumes vast amounts of electricity. As AI becomes more deeply integrated into various sectors, from healthcare to logistics, the energy requirements will skyrocket. To support this future, there must be significant investment in energy infrastructure, particularly in renewable energy sources that can sustainably power these AI systems. Without a reliable and abundant energy supply, the dream of superintelligent AI could be limited by resource constraints, stalling its potential impact.

Data centers, the physical locations where AI systems store and process information, are another critical piece of infrastructure. As AI grows more advanced, these data centers will need to expand in size and capacity to handle the increasing demands. This means not only building more data centers but also making them more efficient in terms of energy use and processing power. The scale of these facilities will likely need to grow exponentially to keep up with AI's data needs. These centers must also be strategically located across the globe to ensure that AI systems can operate with low latency and high reliability, serving users everywhere, regardless of their location.

However, the massive infrastructure needed to support AI also raises concerns about accessibility and equality. Altman acknowledges that if AI becomes a scarce resource controlled by only a few, it could lead to a dangerous concentration of power. Without careful planning, the future of AI could end up in the hands of a small number of corporations or governments with the resources to build and maintain the necessary infrastructure. This would exacerbate existing inequalities, creating a technological divide between those who have access to AI and those who do not.

Altman stresses the importance of ensuring that AI remains accessible to all, avoiding the concentration of power and resources in the hands of the elite. To prevent this, there must be policies and initiatives in place to democratize access to AI technology. This could involve open-source AI platforms, government funding for infrastructure in underdeveloped regions, and partnerships between public and private sectors to distribute the benefits of AI more equitably. If only a few entities control AI's development and deployment, the technology's potential to improve global living standards and solve humanity's problems could be undermined.

One way to avoid this technological divide is to prioritize infrastructure investment in regions that are typically underserved by tech innovation. By building data centers and energy infrastructure in these areas, AI's benefits can reach a broader population. Additionally, open collaboration between governments, industries, and academic institutions can help ensure that AI development is not dominated by a single player. Altman believes that to truly usher in the Intelligence Age, AI must be a tool that everyone can access, not just those with the resources to control it.

In this new era, where AI is poised to reshape the world, infrastructure is the foundation upon which everything rests. The need for computational power, energy resources, and data centers is undeniable, but just as important is ensuring that these resources are shared fairly. By focusing on both the technical and social aspects of AI infrastructure, Altman's vision of the future can be one of widespread prosperity, where the benefits of AI reach across borders and social classes, avoiding a future where AI's power is limited to the privileged few.

Conclusion

Sam Altman's vision for the future, centered around superintelligent AI, paints a bold and ambitious picture of what humanity could achieve. Throughout this journey, we've explored the transformative potential of AI, from personal AI teams that enhance individual decision-making to the sweeping economic shifts AI could bring by optimizing industries and creating new markets. Altman's belief in the Intelligence Age signals the dawn of a new era where AI not only helps solve everyday challenges but also tackles humanity's most complex problems—climate change, space colonization, and scientific discovery. At its core, Altman's vision is one of hope, where AI drives prosperity and enables human progress at unprecedented scales.

However, this future depends on more than just technological advancements. As society moves toward an AI-driven world, there are critical steps that must be taken to ensure that AI's benefits are shared widely and its risks are managed responsibly. Infrastructure must scale to meet the growing demands for computational power, energy, and data storage, while governments and organizations must work together to ensure that AI remains accessible to all, preventing its concentration in the hands of a few. Ethical considerations, transparency, and security must be at the forefront of AI's development to build trust and prevent harm. Furthermore, as the labor market shifts, education and reskilling efforts will be crucial to help people adapt to the changes brought about by AI-driven automation.

As we look to the future, it's worth asking: Can AI truly deliver on the promises that visionaries like Altman have laid out? While AI holds incredible potential, there are significant challenges ahead, from the limitations of deep learning to the risks of job displacement and inequality. Can we trust AI to solve humanity's biggest problems, or will we find that the technology has limits we don't yet understand? These questions invite us to reflect on whether we should proceed with caution, ensuring that the race for AI development does not outpace our ability to manage its consequences.

In the end, the future of AI is not set in stone, but its impact on our world is undeniable. Whether AI will deliver a utopian future of abundance and innovation or one marked by challenges and disruption depends largely on how we navigate this moment. As readers, staying informed about AI's development, understanding its potential impact, and engaging in conversations about its ethical implications will be critical as we move forward. The choices we make today will shape the Intelligence Age and determine whether AI becomes a tool for universal good or a technology that benefits only a few. Now is the time to embrace AI's possibilities while also ensuring that its power is wielded wisely, for the benefit of all humanity.

www.ingramcontent.com/pod-product-compliance
Lightning Source LLC
La Vergne TN
LVHW051617050326
832903LV00033B/4540